HELP FROM ABOVE

Bishop Wale Adekoya

First Printing Year 2007
Second Printing Year 2014
Printed in Federal Republic of Nigeria

Published & Printed By:
Nile Ventures
26, Michael Adekoya Street,
Ilupeju Estate Lagos.
Tel: 08023327260, 08068168909

CONTENTS

ACKNOWLEDGEMENT

I acknowledge the help of the Holy Spirit the Ultimate Helper for his Inspiration and wisdom in writing this book. May I never lose your presence all the days of my life.

<u>DEDICATION</u>

This book is dedicated to men and women who the lord has used as Helping Hands for my ministry. Let God send help to your lives and Families in Jesus name.

PREFACE

That you are holding this book right now is not an accident, it is a divine appointment by God for a definite divine encounter and turn around for your life. This book came into being by the Supernatural hand of God upon my life to inspire me and package this book for your God ordained breakthrough. According to God's promise to me if you will prayerfully and diligently read through this book and carryout the instructions contained in it, also aggressively praying the prophetic prayer points you MUST experience a turn around in your life and situations. I implore you don't rush through or read traditionally but open your heart and listen attentively to what the spirit will communicate to your spirit man, then you can be sure of an encounter with God. The voice of the Lord will come to you as you read. I pray that the Lord will surprise you. Please get across to me and share your testimonies and experiences.

Rev. Wale Adekoya

Tel: 01 8110944, 08033258648

11, Fola Jinadu Crescent, Off Oguntona Crescent,

1st Pedro B/Stop, Gbagada Phase 1, Lagos.
Email: **Shalom_ministries@yahoo.com**
Website www.Shallomintlministries.tripod.com

CHAPTER ONE

WHAT IS DIVINE HELP?

Ps 121:1 -end. "I will lift up my eyes to the Hills from whence cometh my help. My help will come from the Lord, which made the Heavens and the Earth. He will not suffer thy foot to be moved: he that keepeth thee will not slumber. Behold, he that keepeth Israel shall neither slumber nor sleep. The Lord is thy shade upon thy right hand. The sun shall not smite thee by day or by night. The Lord shall preserve thee from all evil: he shall preserve thy soul. The Lord shall preserve thy going out and thy coming in from this time hence forth, and even for evermore."

Ps 60:11 "Give us help from Trouble for the help of man is useless"

The Greatness and Success of every man on earth can be traced to the help of the Almighty God. What makes a difference in any man is the place of Divine Help that is available to such a man. If there is anything you need to seek after it is the Help that comes from above and not from abroad. Many have lived a miserable and frustrated life because they didn't know how to secure the Help that comes from above.

Help means to join and contribute to the performance or completion of a task, project or business venture and ministry.

Help means to make easier, to assist, to remove the burden or stress of accomplishing a goal or vision.

Regeneration and Redemption makes divine help our heritage and possession but obviously we must know how to fully appropriate the help that is available for us. Lack of knowledge has made many to live frustrated lives even when their lot is continual help. David declared in the book of psalms, my help comes from the Lord the maker of Heaven and earth and as a result of this divine help he enumerated the blessings and benefits that have come to him.

David's declaration shows that he has the right perspective and vision. Where are you looking to for help man or God? Look up to God and not man and your help will come speedily. The help of man is vain and useless. Only the almighty God has the power to help you in life and ministry.

> ***Ps 34:5***
> ***"They looked unto him and were lightened and their faces were not ashamed"***

If you look to man you will be ashamed. The Hill represents the place of worship in Jerusalem where God's presence abide. This psalm is a song of ascent, always sang when they are going to the temple. So your help can only come from the presence of the Lord
David spoke with confidence and faith in the help of God. Where is your faith and confidence, for you to receive divine help you need to have faith and confidence in the ability of God.

From Psalm 121, we see the benefits of Divine help which includes:

1. Divine Protection.
2. Divine Presence
3. Divine Peace
4. Divine Preservation
5. Divine Provision

The Knowledge of what is available for you is very important.

Hosea 4:6.
"My People are destroyed for lack of knowledge: because thou hast rejected knowledge, I will also reject thee, that thou shalt be no priest to me: seeing thou hast forgotten the law of thy God, I will also forget thy children."

There are various levels or Realms of Help available to the child of God and there are keys on how to tap into them. I declare that help is coming your way today in Jesus name. Our God is called the very present help in times of trouble, you are not to pass through life struggling and suffering because help is available for you. When divine help locates a person failure is turned to success and accomplishment becomes very easy.

Isaiah 41:10
"Fear thou not; for I am thy God: I will strengthen thee; yea I will help thee; yea, I will uphold thee with the right hand of my Righteousness."

God has Promised to help you and this help right early.

Ps 46:5
"God is in the midst of her; she shall help her and that right early."

Help Right Early is coming your way today in Jesus name. You have struggled enough, it is your time for help from above. Your Season of Help is now. Receive it now and you will testify.

> ***Right early help is help at the appropriate time. No delay or procrastination. It is you been there at the right time.***

PRAYER POINTS

1. I Command that every yoke of frustration over my life be destroyed.
2. Father from Heaven above send Help to me Today in Jesus name.
3. Every hindrance and barrier to my help be destroyed today.
4. Father order my steps to where help is waiting for me.
5. Holy Spirit open my eyes to see my Source of Divine Help.
6. Helpers of My Destiny locate me by Fire in Jesus name.
7. Open my Understanding to the Truth of your word today.
8. Father connect me today with the Right People in Jesus name.
9. By the mercy of God, doors of help open for me in Jesus name.
10. Favour before my Helpers rest upon me now.

CHAPTER TWO

RESULTS OF DIVINE HELP

Ps 46:1
"God is our refuge and strength, a very present help in times of trouble."

Divine help brings a man out of trouble and prisons of life. Joseph came out of the prison by help of the butler who mentioned him to Pharaoh and thereby he entered the palace. God is bringing you into your palace today. There is no self help made man, we all have received help from one person or the other. For us to get to where we are right now. The story of David's getting to the throne cannot be complete without the role of Jonathan in his life. Through the Scriptures we see wonderful stories of how men received Divine help and the glory of their destiny manifested. What you need is Divine help. In your career, ministry or daily pursuit you need divine help. Supernatural help is what makes a man to be better than the other. That is what is lacking in your life. But today your story is changing because God is sending help your way.

SEVEN BENEFITS OF DIVINE HELP

1. Victory is assured when there is divine help. Battles are won by the help of the Lord.

   Isaiah 41:10
   "Fear thou not; for I am with thee; be not dismayed for I am your God; I will strengthen thee; yea I will help thee, yea I would uphold thee with the right hand of my Righteousness."

   Psalms 33:16, 20
   "There is no king saved by the multitude of an host, a mighty is not deliver by the much strength. Our soul waiteth for the Lord, He is our help and our shield"

   > ***You cannot win the battles of life by your strength. You need the help of Jehovah".***

   2nd Chronicles 25:8
   "But if thou wilt go, do it, be strong for the battle: God shall make thee fall

before the enemy: for God hath power to help, and to cast down."

Days of trouble always comes to every man. But at such days and time. You need the help of God. Holy Spirit is that helper . Are you in relationship with him? Do you know his voice?

2. Deliverance in the day of Trouble or contrary circumstances.

Ps 46:1
"God is our refuge and strength, a very present help in trouble."

Ps 20:1-2
"The lord hear thee in the day of trouble; the name of the God of Jacob defend thee ;send thee help from the Sanctuary, and strengthen thee out of Zion."

> ***Help comes from the sanctuary to those who are regular in the sanctuary. Have you visited His presence today?***

3. Divine Provision

Heb 4:16
"Let us therefore come boldly unto the throne of grace, that we may obtain mercy, and find grace to help in time of need.

Needs are met as a result of the overflow of God's Grace. Divine help brings Grace

All needs are supplied when there is divine help.

4. Accomplishments and Success.

2nd Chronicles 26:15
And he made in Jerusalem engines, invented by cunning men, to be on the towers and upon the bulwarks, to shoot arrows and great stones withal. And his name spread far abroad; for he was marvelousy helped, till he was strong

Uzziah was able to accomplish because God helped him, Marvelously Help is your portion today in Jesus name.

5. Spiritual Strength and Success.

Romans 8:26
"Likewise the spirit also helpeth our infirmities: for we know not what we should pray for as we ought: but the Spirit itself makes intercession for us with groanings that cannot be uttered."

Our weakness is replaced with strength when Divine help comes. The word infirmities means weakness. The Holy Spirit can help and strengthen your prayer life.

6. Protection and Security

Ps 121:1- 3.
"I will lift mine eyes up to the hills, from whence cometh my help. My help cometh from the Lord who made the Heavens and the Earth. He would not suffer my foot to be moved".

Your eternal security and protection is quaranted through Divine help

7. Divine Presence

Ps 46:1
"God is our refuge and strength, a very present help in trouble.

Divine presence is the key to Divine comfort. Today make a decision to seek for his divine help in your daily walk with the Lord.

PRAYER POINTS

1. Father I release angelic help to fight the invisible battles of my life.
2. I release Supernatural help upon my life for financial breakthrough.
3. Help from above locate me today.
4. Anointing for Divine help fall upon me today.
5. Lord baptize me with Favour for uncommon help.
6. You my helpers remember me for good today.
7. I raise an altar for divine help for my business in Jesus name.
8. Satanic gathering against my help scatter by fire in Jesus name.
9. Holy Spirit send help to my prayer life for Spiritual breakthrough.
10. Rivers of Divine Help flow into my life today in Jesus name.
11. I Prophesy Divine Help into every area of my Life.
12. Help from above encompasss me today by fire.

CHAPTER THREE

LEVELS OF HELP

There are different levels of help that can come to a person. It is my prayer that you will begin to experience help at this various levels. You need all round help for all round blessing and breakthrough in your life. Each level of help will produce different results in your life. You need to understand how each stream of help will flow towards you. The key that will unlock each flow of help will be revealed to you and your obedience will plug you into the flow of all around help. Obedience is the mother of all divine help.

LEVELS OF HELP

There are five levels of help I have discovered in the word of God.

1. Holy Spirit -Ultimate Helper.
2. Angelic Help and assistance.
3. Prophetic Helping Hands.
4. Human angelic Helpers.

5. Enemies turned to Helpers.

These five levels of help represent the major foundation for help and that is the Grace of God. Five is the number for Grace.

> ***Hebrews 4:16***
> ***"Let us therefore come boldly unto the throne of grace, that we may obtain mercy, and find grace to help in time of need."***

Helps comes to us as a result of the outflow of God's Grace. We are not worthy of the help of God but his Grace made help available to us as we were drown in sin and filthiness by bringing Salvation to everyman.

> ***Titus 2:11***
> ***"For the grace of God that bringeth salvation hath appeared to all men".***

1. HOLY SPIRIT: - THE ULTIMATE HELPER

The Holy Spirit is called the helper in the scriptures. The Greek word paracletos is translated into seven words of which one of it is that he is our helper. The word paracletos is translated Holy Spirit

John 14:15 17
" I f y e l o v e m e , k e e p m y commandments and I will pray the Father, and he shall give you another helper that he may abide with you forever."

I will pray the father and he will give you another helper.

The word paracletos means one called alongside i.e. to take the place of Jesus. The Lord Jesus Christ was the First Helper sent by the Father but he will give you another helper the Holy Spirit. He will abide with you forever.

THE MINISTRY OF HELP OF THE HOLY SPIRIT

Until you begin to experience the ministry of the Holy Spirit in your life, things are going to be hard for you. The struggle will continue and breakthrough becomes very difficult.

In fact without the help of the Spirit you cannot live successfully in your Christian Life. He is the very present help in time of trouble as revealed in Ps 46 vs 1

In what way will he help you?

1. He will guide you into all truth. John 14:26.
2. He would show you things to come.
3. He will teach you all you need to know.
4. He will help you in your prayer life. Rom 8:26
5. He will help you in living above sin. Rom 8
6. He will help with winning Souls. Acts 1:8
7. He will help you with Spiritual Gifts. 1Cor 12
8. He will help you by imparting fruits of the Spirit. Gal 5:21.
9. He will help you with Ministry Gifts. Eph 4:11

I cannot recount all the testimonies that this wonderful personality has performed in my life and ministries. At different difficult situations in my life I have received his help and assistance. The greatest prayer for me is that whisper under my breath "Help me Holy Spirit". I have seen great doors open, great favour and help, direction and guidance, breakthrough in my Life and ministries. I have seen people change their minds and decisions by uttering that short phrase at desperate points in my life. In my daily walk and pursuit I have seen marvelous help by calling for the help of the Holy Spirit at different circumstances. From today you will begin to see his help and manifestations in your life more than ever before. He desires so much to help you because he has been sent by the master Jesus Christ to be your Ultimate helper.

HOW DO YOU RECEIVE HIS MINISTRY OF HELP

1. Be sincerely born again. If you have not given him your life, please you can do it now just pray this prayer now:

   Father I repent of my sins and ask you to come into my life. I accept you today as my Lord and Saviour. I believe you died for me on Calvary cross, save my soul today and write my name in the book of Life.

2. Please read the following Scriptures to know the character of the Holy Spirit.
   John chapter 14 and 16, 1st Corinthians 12, 13 and 14. Knowing His character will help you to relate with him and so be able to enjoy his ministry

3. Regularly fellowship and commune with the Holy Spirit on a daily basis. To commune means to talk and ask the Holy Spirit for daily help.

   2 Cor. 13:14
   "The grace of the Lord Jesus

Christ, and the love of God, and the communion of the Holy Ghost be with you all. Amen"

4. Spend time in Praise and Worship and live a Praiseful Life. Praise is the atmosphere for the Holy Spirit to move in your life, remove bitterness, complaining, murmuring, anxiety and worry.

   Ephesians 4: 30-32
   "And grieve not the Holy Spirit of God, whereby ye are sealed unto the day redemption, let all bitterness, and wrath, and anger, and clamour, and evil speaking, be put away from you, with all malice, and be ye kind one to another, tenderhearted forgiving one another, even as God for Christ's sake hath forgiven you."

5. Learn to ask for help and assistance in your daily endeavours. You have to ask him before he will respond to you. Don't forget he is a gentle personality and will never intrude until you ask him.

PRAYER POINTS

1. Father baptize me today with the Power of the Holy Spirit.
2. Holy Spirit I enter into a deep relationship with you today.
3. I make a covenant with you Holy Spirit today to receive your daily help.
4. I receive the Supernatural help of the Holy Spirit today for Breakthrough.
5. Holy Spirit move in my life for Divine Help.

2. ANGELIC HELP

2Kings 19:35
"And it came to pass that night that the angel of the Lord went out, and smote in the camp of the Assyrians an hundred score and five thousand:

The next level of help is angelic help and assistance All through we see different people of God experience angelic assistance through protection, deliverance, provision, breakthrough and victory. In this passage above we see the angel of the Lord fight for the children of Israel and make them victorious. We also know how Peter was delivered from prison through angelic assistance.

Ps 34:7,

" The angel of the Lord emcampeth round about them that fear him, and delivereth them",

Heb. 1:13-14

"But to which of the angels said he at any time, sit on my right hand, until I make thine enemies thy foot-stool, are they not all ministering spirit, sent forth to minister for them who shall be heirs of salvation"

Acts 12:7-8.

"And, behold, the angel of the Lord came upon him, and a light shined in the prison: and he smote Peter on the side, and raised him up saying. Arise up quickly. And his chains fell from his hands, And the angel said unto him, Gird thyself, and bind on thy sandals. And so he did. And he saith unto him, Cast thy garment about thee, and follow me."

I have at several times experience angelic assistance in my trips within and outside the nation. Several times we were delivered from motor accident by angelic interventions. I have had several revelations and seeing angelic assistance released to me for Spiritual Warfares and breakthroughs. Brethren angelic help is very real and possible today.

1. You have to believe God for it and be expectant in your daily pursuit.
2. You have to ask for angelic assistance in times of trouble and difficulty.
3. Always ask in the name of Jesus Christ the Lord of the Hosts of Heaven.
   Angels have been sent by God to minister to you and help you but you have to take advantage of them

PRAYER POINTS

1. I release Angelic Assistance to go forth and fight the battles of my Life.
2. In the name of Jesus I command Angels of Protection to watch over my Family and Property.
3. You Angels of Deliverance I release you now to deliver me from every prison the enemy has kept me.
4. Every of my inheritance stolen by the enemy be released through angelic assistance.
5. I release angels of Heaven to go ahead and make a way for my breakthrough.

6. Let the angels of the lord pursue, overtake and recover all my blessings
7. Every battle surrounding my breakthrough I release the Host of Heaven to Fight for me today.
8. I command angels of God to slay every giant of delay in my life in Jesus name.
9. I decree that angels of God will uproot every demonic blockage on my way to greatness in Jesus name.
10. I release Warring Angels to fight and demolish every wall of limitation raised by the enemy.

3. PROPHETIC HELPING HAND

2nd Chronicles 20:20

"And they arose early in the morning, and went forth into the wilderness of Tekoa: and as they went forth, Jehoshaphat stood and said, hear me, O Judah, and ye Jerusalem; believe in the Lord your God, so shall ye be established; believe his prophets, so shall ye prosper."

Isaiah 44:26
"That confirmeth the word of his servant, and performeth the counsel of his messengers; that saith to Jerusalem, thou shalt be inhabited and to the cities of Judah, ye shall be built, and I will raise up the decayed places thereof:"

God has not changed in his ways of doing things. He has raised men in the land to help you possess and fulfill your destiny. There are men and women of God who are genuinely anointed to help you in fulfilling your purpose here on earth. It is very important for you to recognize that they are raised by God for your lifting and greatness. You are therefore expected to embrace their ministry and follow their instructions. One instruction from the man of God can make a difference and remove every struggle in your life. Several examples in the scriptures reveal this truth. The role of Elijah in the life of the woman of Zarephath could be mentioned.

1Kings 17:13-16
"And Elijah said unto her, Fear not; go and do as thou hast said: but make me thereof a little cake first, and bring it unto me, and after for thee and for thy son, for thus saith the LORD the

barrel of meal shall not waste, neither shall the cruse of oil fail, until the day that the LORD sendeth rain upon the earth,"

Elijah was the prophetic helping hand to deliver the woman from the famine that came upon the land. Also the story of the woman in

2Kings 4:1-3

"Now there cried a certain woman of the wives of the son of the prophets unto Elisha, saying, Thy servant my husband is dead; and thou knowest that thy servant did fear the LORD: and the creditor is come to take unto him my two sons to the bondmen, and Elisha said unto her , what shall I do for thee? tell me what hast thou in the house? And she said, Thine handmaid hath not any thing in the house, save a pot of oil, then he said, Go, borrow thee vessels abroad of all thy neighbours, even empty vessels,

How she was delivered from debt and financial embarrassment cannot but be a miracle of God, so you have to understand that there are men God will send your way to help you overcome in the battles of life. God confirms the pronouncement of his ministers. Had Naaman rejected the instruction of Elisha he would have remained in his leprosy forever. Prophets are God sent. They are God's helping hands to the Church. They have their ears next to God's mouth. God speaks through them, putting prophetic words into their mouths that affect men's destinies. However there are fake prophets but by their fruits you shall know them.

Proclamation receive this prophetic words, I proclaim that every warfare raging against you right now be quenched in Jesus name.

From now, God will stir up the hearts of Kings and nobles to favour you.
I release your breakthrough now in Jesus name.

I command every affliction and Struggle to come to an end now in Jesus name.

You have a responsibility to believe and receive a man of God, God is sending your way. Also you have a strong responsibility to celebrate the grace on his or her life. And you can't start nursing ill feelings about him or her and expect to prosper by his ministry. You have to humble yourself and believe his prophets for you to prosper. Also you have to sow your seed of Finance and Favour into his life.

We have several examples of that in the scriptures. The woman of Zarephath gave her last meal to Elijah before her breakthrough. Let God lead you in sowing your seed of favour to a mentor or prophetic minister that God has sent your way and you will never regret doing so.

PRAYER POINTS

1. Father send your messenger my way carrying a word of deliverance for my breakthrough.
2. Father connect me with your vessel that will lift up my hand spiritually and help me to accomplish my destiny.
3. Open the eyes of my understanding to the secrets of the kingdom.
4. Holy Spirit grant me the next instruction for my next level promotion.
5. Open my heart to receive prophetic instructions from your own servant.
6. Send your servant my way that will prophetically accelerate my speed for success.
7. Confirm the pronouncements of your servants concerning my destiny.
8. Every power hindering God's prophetic promise for my life be destroyed.
9. By spirit of prophecy I decree my immediate turn around in Jesus name.

10. I lay claim to every God's prophetic word spoken into my life and I command their fulfillment.

4. HUMAN ANGELIC HELPERS

Many have climbed the shoulders of others to get to the top. Relationships with the right person can accelerate your destiny. There are men God will send your way to promote your destiny. You need to have discernment and wisdom to harness the potential of such relationships. All through the scriptures we have various examples of such human angelic helpers. In the story of the greatness of Joseph we know the role played by the butler in recommending Joseph to Pharaoh. This eventually led to Joseph getting to the throne in Egypt.

> ***Gen 41:9 -14***
> ***"Then spake the chief butler unto pharaoh saying, I do remember my faults this day. Pharaoh was wroth with his servants, and put me in ward in the captain of the guard's house, both me and the chief baker. And we dreamed a dream in one night, I and he; we dreamed each man according to the interpretation of his dream. And there was there***

with us a young man, an Hebrew, servant to the captain of the guard; and we told him, and he interpreted to us our dreams; to each man according to his dream he did interpret. And it came to pass, as he interpreted to us so it was, me he restored unto mine office, and him he hanged.

Then pharaoh sent and called Joseph, and they brought him hastily out of the dungeon and he shaved himself, and changed his raiment, and came in unto pharaoh."

Also I am sure you remember the story of David and Jonathan. Jonathan actually paved the way for David's getting to the throne of Israel.

1 Sam 20:1 -4.

"And David fled from Naioth in Ramah; we came and said before Jonathan, what have I done? What is mine iniquity? And what is my sin before thy father, that he seeketh my life? and said unto him, God forbid; thou shalt not die: behold, my father will do nothing either great or small, but that he will shew it and

why should my father hide this thing from me? It is not so and David sware moreover, and said, thy father certainly knowth that I have found grace in thine eyes; and he saith, let not Jonathan know this, lest he be grieved: but truly, as the Lord liveth, and as thy soul liveth, there is but a step between me and death. Then said Jonathan unto David, whatsoever thy soul desireth, I will even do it for thee".

I prophesy that your helper will locate you this month. The Jonathan of your destiny will manifest to you. There are human helpers sent by God to help you in the journey to greatness. I have several experiences in my life about such helpers. My breakthrough into the international ministry was through a helper who God sent my way at the appropriate time. What I have tried to do over years happened overnight in an easy way. Several doors have been opened to me by various men and women God has sent my way to assist me. There are several keys that will help you to harness such helpers.

Prob. 27:17
"Iron sharpeneth iron; so a man sharpeneth the countenance of his friend."

WHAT YOU MUST DO

1. You must develop and maintain relationship with the right people.
2. Character and attitude can be of great help.
3. Sacrifice is the key to maintaining relationships.
4. Never look down on people or underestimate what God can do through people.
5. Humble yourself to ask for help and assistance when you need.
6. Always ask God to anoint you with favour

PRAYER POINTS.

1. Helpers of destiny manifest for me today in Jesus name.
2. Holy Ghost connect me today with men you have ordained to favour me.
3. Every garment of disfavour on my life be destroyed in Jesus name.
4. Oil of favour fall upon me today in Jesus name.
5. Every spirit of procrastination working in the life of my helpers be destroyed in Jesus name.
6. I release my divine helpers to come forth.
7. Every veil over my life hindering my divine connection be consumed by fire.

8. Doors of divine connection open for me by fire in Jesus name.
9. Lord disarrange all my enemies and arrange me for divine connection.
10. Chains of delay in my life break by fire in Jesus name.

YOUR WIFE: HEAVEN ORDAINED HELPER

> ***Gen 2:18***
> ***"And the Lord said, it is not good that the man should be alone; I will make him a help meet for him."***

Your wife is one of the helpers that God has given you as a child of God. The bible calls your wife your helpmate. She is incomparable to none, she is a help suitable to man intellectually, morally and physically, as his counterpart. Most partners underestimate the role of their spouse in helping them achieving their God given destiny and purpose. Infact there is no one to be compared to your spouse as a helper. But obviously you have to invest in your spouse for him/her to play the role effectively and wonderfully. Power of agreement that can come to play in your prayer life cannot be overemphasized. That power of agreement can overcome every obstacles, mountains and trials of life. She or he is your best counselor, consoler, encourager, strengthener and supporter. If nobody else believes your vision your spouse can and must believe your vision. The greatest key to your success is to be able to maximize the potential of your spouse as your helper. Don't overlook it, you have to do all that you know to put your spouse in a position of truly being your helper because that is God's plan for your success. Many men will tell you the deep testimonies of how their wives have been the source of their success and achievement today. Most of the great achievers of today cannot hide from this fact that their achievement was because of their spouse. So please work on your relationship with your spouse so that the desired success can be achieved.

STEPS TO TAKE

1. Pray to God to give you the right spouse also patiently and prayerfully choose the right spouse for your destiny.
2. Invest your time, love, and resources into developing your spouse to be the kind of partner you want her to be.
3. openness, transparency, trust and humility are vital factors that will help to make him or her fulfill the role of helper in your life e.g. most men that are not humble enough to listen to advice from their wives may be missing a great help in that area. He or she is a major

stakeholder in your destiny so understand this.

4. Always carry him or her along the way in the journey to greatness. He or she is the closest person to you.
5. Learn to forgive and forget his/her failures and move on in life.

PRAYER POINTS

1. Father heal my marriage today of every past wounds and restore true love to my marriage.
2. Jehovah touch my spouse and make him or her true helper to me in Jesus name.
3. I command the spirit of love and unity to begin to reign in my marriage.
4. Open my eyes to see the great potential in my spouse and to maximize them.
5. I release my spouse from every evil or contrary influence hindering his or her Biblical role in this marriage.
6. Anointing for him/her to function as my helper let it fall upon her.
7. Lord perfect that which concerns my marriage today in Jesus name.

6. <u>ENEMIES TURNED TO HELPERS</u>

Prov 16:7
"When a man's ways please the LORD, he maketh even his enemies to be at peace with him."

God in his Supernatural way have times without number turned enemies to become helpers for his people. He has also turned the evil plans of the enemy to become helps for his people to accomplish greatness. That is why as a child of God never allow your circumstances to make you bitter. Strange people have gone out of their way to help God's people in a way that has dazed people. In Isaiah 45, King Cyrus was a gentile King who God decided to use to help bring deliverance and breakthrough to the children of Israel. The children of Israel received their greatest favour and abundant provision from the Egyptians who had greatly punished and enslaved them for 400 years. One day of favour made a difference in the life of God's people. They spoiled the Egyptians and came out of Egypt with so much wealth that they had never received. God is awesome in power and can turn your enemies to become your helpers in his own Supernatural way. The evil plan of Joseph's brothers became the needed help for him to get to his place of fulfillment in destiny. As a child of God never be bitter towards anyone and always maintain a heart of forgiveness to all.

> ***Gen 50:19 - 21.***
> ***"And Joseph said unto them, fear not: for am I in the place of God? But as for you, ye thought evil against me; but God meant it unto good, to bring to pass, as it is this day, to save much people alive. Now therefore fear ye not: I will nourish you, and your little ones. And he comforted them, and spake kindly unto them."***

It was Haman the enemy of mordecai who announced to the king what he should do to honour mordecai. He never knew that the advice he gave to the king was for mordecai"

Note the following instructions that will help your Journey to greatness.

1. Always learn to forget the past it has no life. Keep no records of wrong doings and evil.
2. "Count it all Joy when you fall into divers trials and tribulations" James 1:2.
3. Walk in love with all men.
4. be open and receptive to the move of God in your life.

PRAYER POINTS.

1. Father overturn the plans of the enemies and bring glory to your name.
2. Father let every event in my life bring blessing and progress to my life.
3. You enemies of progress receive a new heart today.
4. Let every evil plans of the enemies become my stepping stones to promotion in Jesus name.
5. Jehovah the man of war fight the battle of my life and grant me victory.
6. Let every Haman of my life be disgraced in Jesus name.
7. Jehovah the man of war, fight for me today in Jesus name.
8. Invisible battles surrounding my breakthrough be destroyed.
9. Father let every secret plot of the enemy be to my favour.
10. Let your judgment come upon every Haman in my life.

CHAPTER FOUR

SATANIC BARRIERS TO RECEIVING DIVINE HELP

Ephesians 6:11
"Put on the whole armour of God that ye may be able to stand against the wiles of the devil"

2 Cor. 2:11
"Lest Satan should get an advantage of us for we are not ignorant of his devices"

In the above passages it is obvious that Satan has devices, wiles, strategies, schemes or activities that he uses to hinder the children of God. We are told not to be ignorant. Many are ignorant of the devices of the devil and so the devil takes advantage of them by hindering them from their help. We need the spirit of discernment and knowledge of the devices of the enemy to be able to overcome. But the truth is this for you to experience divine help you need to practice spiritual warfare and stand against the wiles of the wicked in aggressive prayers and fasting. Some of the devices of the wicked comes in various ways and patterns. I decree today victory shall be your portion in Jesus name.

I will be revealing to you some of those devices but you need to tackle them in serious prayers and don't take things for granted.

1. SATANIC RESISTANCE

> ***Zech 3:1***
> ***"And he shewed me Joshua the high priest standing before the angels of the Lord and Satan standing at his right hand to resist him"***

There are people who experience Satanic resistance. The enemy resist anything good coming their way. People will always approve their helpers from helping them . If the helper tries to help, he finds a lot of opposition in his trying to help this person. In the Board room somebody is there resisting his promotion or the contract that is about to be awarded to him. If you find all manners of opposition to your breakthrough please pray this prayers:-

1. Every power of Satanic resistance in and

around my life be scattered in Jesus name.

2. Circle of Satanic resistance be scattered by fire in Jesus name.
3. You agents of opposition to my breakthrough
be paralysed in Jesus name.
4. Stronghold of Satanic resistance crumble by fire in Jesus name.
5. Jehovah the man of war fight every invisible battle confronting me in Jesus name.

2. SATANIC DIVERSION

This happens that what has been promised you is given to someone else. The enemy diverts people's blessings and help by arranging someone else to come and claim the blessings. You are looking for a Job and they tell you, they have been looking for you but they couldn't find you and so they gave the Job or the contract to someone else. That is Satanic diversion at work. The money that has been kept for you is now diverted and used for another purpose because you came too late or you were no where to be found or something happened that made the person who promised you to use the money for another purpose. If this happens to you regularly pray the following prayers aggresively.

1. You powers diverting my blessings and inheritance be paralysed in Jesus name.

2. From today my help shall not be diverted again in Jesus name.
3. Oh Lord order my steps to be at the right place and at the right time.
4. Every evil wind blowing against my help, be still in Jesus name.
5. Every Satanic arrangement diverting my blessings scatter in Jesus name.

3. SATANIC ATTACKS ON YOUR HELPERS

Dan. 10:12-13
"Then said he unto me, Fear not, Daniel: for from the first day that thou didst set thine heart to understand, and to chasten thyself before thy God, thy words were heard, and I am come for thy word. But the prince of the kingdom of Persia withstood me one and twenty days: but lo, Michael, one of the chief princes, came to help me; and I remained there with the kings of Persia"

There are times when any one that promise you help will always experience attack or misfortune and will have to fail in his promise to you. People promise and fail because after they promise you they experience attack on their finances, business, carrier or health. Thereby this your helpers are now helpless in their situation that they cannot fulfil their promise to you. Somebody promise to help get a Job and then before you know he has been sacked. If you have recurrent events like this you must pray aggressively to contend with the enemy. The man who promised to help in your marital plans has just been sacked or lost his wife or even more worse lost his life. Pray this prayer aggressively.

1. Every attack on my potential helpers be destroyed in Jesus name .
2. Satanic plans concerning my helpers be cancelled today in Jesus name.
3. Failure at the edge of Breakthrough be terminated in Jesus name.
4. Arrows of failure released against my helpers back fire in Jesus name.
5. You my Helpers receive Divine Covering in Jesus name.

4. SATANIC BLACKMAIL

Nehemaih 4:7-9

But it came to pass, that when Saballat, and Tobiah, and the Arabians, and Ammonites, and the

Ashdodites, heard that the walls of Jerusalem were made up, and that the breaches began to be stopped, then they were very wroth. And conspired all of them together to come and to fight against Jerusalem, and to hinder it. Nevertheless we made our prayer unto our God, and set a watch against them day and night, because of them.

Study Nehemiah chapters 4 to 6 very well and you will see how Tobiah and Sanbailat conspired and plotted to destroy the divine help Nehemiah received to build the walls of Jerusalem. They try to blackmail them by carrying a negative news to the king and others.

The enemy does that, at the point of breakthrough or promotion. He raises an evil reports, or create a negative rumour around town concerning your life or business. You have to be very careful. Read Nehemaih 4:4-5 see the prayers that Nehemiah prayed in those verses. In chapter 6 your will see all the steps they took to hinder Nehemiah from completing the project. But Nehemiah was determined, discerning and dedicated to his God given vision. You have to be like Nehemiah if you are going to be victorious in the battles of life. They even raised false prophets who prophesy to stop the projects and that is why you need to be careful for the kind of prophesy you accept. When the enemy carries evil report about you do not be discouraged but press on to accomplish your goal. Pray this prayers right now.

1. Every evil wind of negative report blowing against my life be still in Jesus name.
2. Every evil tongue speaking against my progress be silenced in shame in Jesus name.
3. Arrows of weariness and weakness released against me back fire in Jesus name.
4. O Lord Arise on my behalf and silence all my persecutors in Jesus name.
5. Helpers of destiny locate me today in Jesus name.

5. SATANIC MANIPULATIONS

The enemy sometime manipulates by painting a wrong picture about you to your helpers. The devil misrepresents you to people by giving them wrong impressions about you to those that are supposed to help you. They begin to see in a negative way. The devil can sometimes cover the person with a wrong image that is been seen by your helpers in the spirit. As a result of this wrong image they are reluctant to help. Or sometimes there is a kind of hatred between you and your helpers. And sometimes you don't even want to do anything with them by the negative

image already created by the enemy. And in many cases the enemy has succeed in completely separating some people from their helpers. They are thousand of miles away from their helpers infact they are going further apart every day that if there is no divine intervention it may be difficult for them to meet. You have to rise up in prayer because God forbid that your helper should pass away then you have a serious issue with God.
Prayer the following prayers.

1. Stronghold of Satanic manipulation in my life be destroyed in Jesus name.
2. Agents of Satanic manipulations be disgraced in Jesus name.
3. Secrets of Satanic manipulation in my life be exposed in Jesus name.
4. Every Satanic manipulation against my help be destroyed by fire.
5. Occultic forces promoting manipulation in my life be frustrated.
6. By your mercy let Destiny helpers favour me in Jesus name.
7. Doors of Divine help open for me in Jesus name.
8. Help from above locate me by fire .
9. Every Satanic arrangement against my help be demolished in Jesus name
10. Annointing for divine help fall upon me.

CHAPTER FIVE

OBSTACLES TO RECEIVING HELP

Deut 28:29
"And thou shalt grope at noonday, as the blind gropeth in darkness, and thou shalt not prosper in thy ways: and thou shalt plant a vineyard, and shalt not gather the grapes therefore."

1. Curses can hinder a man from receiving help. If you have been experiencing disappointments, rejection, hatred struggle and hardship. It may be because there is a curse that is at work in your life that needs to be broken and destroyed. Give yourself to repentance, fasting and prayer and if possible go for proper deliverance ministration so that things can change for you to prosper and succeed.

2. Wrong attitude can hinder you from receiving help. Therefore have the mind of

Christ and the right attitude for your helpers to locate you. Attitudes like pride, lack of integrity, inferiority complex etc. Can hinder help from people.

3. Negative Mind Set ***Prov. 23:7 As a man thinks in his heart so is he.*** Your mind must be renewed with the word of God. Impossibility thinking, discouragement, I cannot mentality, critical mind can hinder you from receiving help.

4. Wrong Appearance. Help can elude you as a result of your appearance. It is important you dress well on all occasions. The way you dress is the way you will be addressed.

5. Trusting man. Never look up to any man for help. Always maintain your focus on God and trust him for all things.

Jeremiah 17:5- 7
"Thus saith the Lord; Cursed be the man that trusteth in man, and maketh flesh his arm, and whose heart departeth from the Lord. For he shall be like the heath in the desert, and shall not see when good cometh; but shall inhabit the parched places in the wilderness, in a salt land and not inhabited. Blessed is the man that

trusteth in the Lord and whose hope the Lord is."

6. Undisciplined Tongue It is important to learn to control your tongue anywhere you are. What you say to people affects the way they respond to you. Believe God to help you say the right things at the right time. When you are before your helper, may God help you say the right words in Jesus name.

   Ps. 39:1
   "I said, I will take heed to my ways that I sin not with my tongue: I will keep my mouth with a bridle, while the wicked is before me".

7. Satanic Hindrances the devil is always at work to hinder and accuse God's people so understand that there is a place of Spiritual warfare for you to posses what belongs to you. 2 Cor. 10:3-5, James 4:7

8. Disobedience: - It is very important for you to live a life of obedience to God's word. Disobedience can hinder you from receiving divine help. Obedience to his instruction prepares you for the blessing of God.

   Isaiah 1:19.
   "If ye be willing and obedient, ye shall eat the good of the land."

CHAPTER SIX

HOW TO SECURE DIVINE HELP

Following the instruction here will bring transformation to your life.

1. Be born again: - You have to truly surrender your life to Jesus Christ so that things can begin to work for the better in your life.

2. Prayer: - Prayer is the key to receiving from the lord. Spend quality time to regularly call for the help of God in all your endeavors and pursuit. If possible add fasting to it. Pray the prayer points in this book and believe God for a turn around in your life.

   Matt 7:7"

   Ask and it shall be given you, seek and ye shall find; knock and it shall be opened unto you."

3. <u>Service:</u>

John 12:26

"If any man serve me, let him follow me; and where I am, there shall also my servants be: if any man serve me, him w i l l my father honour."

You have to locate a place of service in the kingdom for help to locate you. When you are at your location of service your allocation of divine help will meet you. You can't be a bench warmer in the house of the Lord and expect divine help. What are you doing for God? You have to be committed to service in the House of God

4. <u>Humility:-</u>
God always resist the proud and gives grace to the humble. Humility guarantees your lifting in the kingdom of God. H u m i l i t y will qualify you for help before God and men please humble yourself so that he may promote you.

James 4:6
" But he giveth more grace. Wherefore he saith, God resisteth the proud, but giveth grace unto the humble".

5. Sow a seed of Help to Others:-

Gal 6:7- 9
"Be not deceived; God is not mocked: for whatsoever a man soweth that he shall reap. For he that soweth to his flesh reap corruption; but he that soweth to the spirit shall of the spirit reap life everlasting. And let us not be weary in well doing: for in due season we shall reap if we faint not."

Whatever you sow is what you reap. Try to help others and God will make a Harvest of help to come your way. What you make happen for others God will make happen for you.

6. Develop relationships: - relationships make life interesting. So learn to develop good relationships with people, trusting God to use whoever he chooses to use to support you.

Prov 27:17
"Iron sharpens iron: so a man sharpeneth the countenance of his friend."

7. Be faithfull in your tithing and be a giver to Kingdom projects. Favour is released as you give towards the kingdom business, you begin to find favour with men and women. I prophesy help is coming your way in Jesus name. You will never lack help again. This is your season of divine lifting.

PRAYER POINTS

Pray the following prayers aggressively and you will see his mighty hand in your life.

1. Father let your awesome hand for help come upon my life today.
2. Every power frustrating my destiny be destroyed in Jesus name.
3. Helpers of destiny be release for me today in Jesus name.
4. Favour for divine help fall upon me.
5. By your divine help father elevate me today.
6. Satanic embargo over my helpers be cancelled in Jesus name.
7. Doors of divine help open for me today.
8. Every conspiracy against my help today scatter by fire.
9. Every withholding spirit in the life of my helpers be terminated in Jesus name.
10. Every yoke of labour without help be destroyed in Jesus name.

11. Power for divine accomplishment come upon me today.
12. Uncommon help and favour be my portion now in Jesus name.
13. Anointing for start and finish fall upon my life.
14. Every chain of poverty and failure in my life be destroyed by fire.
15. Help from above locate me speedily in Jesus name.
16. Father let there be divine remembrance on my behalf in Jesus name.
17. Every lost opportunity be restored now.
18. Anointing for divine help fall upon me in Jesus name.
19. Help without delay I receive now in Jesus name.
20. Super abundant help shall be my portion in Jesus name.

Begin to thank him for answered prayers.

Worship with us at

SHALOM INTERNATIONAL CHRISTIAN CHURCH
Chapel of Peace

11, fola jinadu crescent off oguntona crescent
1st pedro bus stop Gbagada phase 1 Lagos Nigeria.
Tel: 234.1.8110944, 234.8033258648,
234.1- 8034341963.
U. K. 44-7852389439, USA. 1-5622718692

Email: Shalom_ministries@yahoo.com
Website: www.shalomng.org

Times of Service
Sunday Service:
1st Service Communion Service: 9:00am -10.00am
2nd Service Miracle Service: 10:00am-12:00am

Wednesday Service: Get equipped: 6 -8:00pm

Saturdays: Yoke Destroying Prayer: 7:30-10:00am

Discipleship training Institute:
Mon, Tue, And Thurs: 6 -8pm
Saturdays 10am-3p.m.

Last Friday of the month
Over comers Night Vigil: 11:00pm- 5:00a.m

OTHERS BOOKS BY THE SAME AUTHOR

1. Living By The Word
2. Living The Victorious Christian Life
3. Seeds Of Wisdom On Discipleship
4. Little Instruction Book On Discipleship
5. Keys To Breakthrough In Prayers
6. Walking In His Steps
7. Believers Responsibility
8. Secret Of Discipleship And Disciple Making
9. Power Of Discipline
10. 7 Levels Of Commitment In The Disciple's Life
11. 20 Keys To Open Heavens
12. What Is Divine Help
13. How To Build Disciples & Disciple Makers In The Church
14. Help from Above
15. Releasing your seasons of better things
16. 7 keys to the uncommon blessing
17. 7 Channel of breakthrough prayers
18. Walking in His Glory
19. The Power Of Grace
20. 7 powers in a woman
21. Discipleship - Key to total deliverance
22. 50 Powerful Keys for Financial Abundance with Prophetic Prayer Points
23. 7 Portraits of Real Man and Father.
24. Disciple making Pastor and church Part 1
25. Disciple making Pastor and church Part 2
26. Keys to fruitful and peaceful marriage.
27. Principles of walking in divine favour

www.ingramcontent.com/pod-product-compliance
Lightning Source LLC
LaVergne TN
LVHW040920150826
845672LV00007B/2129

9798353079026